READY, STEADY, PRACTISE!

Jon Goulding

Spelling
Pupil Book **Year 6**

Features of this book

- Clear explanations and worked examples for each spelling topic from the KS2 National Curriculum.

- Questions split into three sections that become progressively more challenging:

Warm up

Test yourself

Challenge yourself

- 'How did you do?' checks at the end of each topic for self-evaluation.

- Regular progress tests to assess pupils' understanding and recap on their learning.

- Answers to every question in a pull-out section at the centre of the book.

Contents

Latin suffixes

Many suffixes originate from Latin. Understanding the meaning of a particular suffix may help you to understand the meaning and spelling of the whole word.

For example: the suffixes **–able** and **–ible** both mean **capable of**.

Comfort**able** means capable of giving comfort.

Ed**ible** means capable of being eaten.

comfort**able**

ed**ible**

Warm up

1 Rewrite these correctly with an **–able** or **–ible** suffix.

Use a dictionary to help you.

fashion	invis
respons	suit
reason	remark
horr	flex

2 Remove the suffix from each of these words and spell the root word correctly.

Use a dictionary to help you.

valuable	reliable
deplorable	movable
memorable	usable

3 Identify the three misspelled words and then write the correct spelling of each word.

horrible	reasonible	identifiable	memorible
responsable	terrible	replaceable	comfortable

4 Here are some more words with common Latin suffixes. Write the root word.
Then write a sentence containing the word with the Latin suffix.

a) leakage

b) assistant

c) gigantic

d) mountaineer

e) familiar

f) signify

g) justice

h) reliable

How did you do?

Prefixes

Some prefixes tell you about numbers.

Examples:

a **uni**corn

uni– means one

a **bi**cycle

bi– means two

a **tri**angle

tri– means three

Warm up

1 What is the correct name for each cycle?

a)

b)

c)

2 Write a definition for each of these words.

Use a dictionary to help you.

a) unicorn

b) unison

c) unify

d) unique

e) biplane

f) binoculars

g) triplets

h) triathlon

i) tripod

3 Match each **bi–** word with its correct meaning.

Use a dictionary if necessary.

bicycle   **bilingual**   **bisect**   **biped**

a) to cut into two parts

b) speaks two languages

c) an animal with two feet

d) a vehicle with two wheels

4 Match each **tri–** word with its correct meaning.

Use a dictionary if necessary.

triangle   **tricycle**   **trio**   **triple**

a) to multiply by three

b) a shape with three sides

c) a group of three

d) a vehicle with three wheels

Challenge yourself

5 Identify the words which use a prefix in the passage below. Then write each word **and** its root word.

> He found it impossible to ride the unicycle because he was incapable of riding a bicycle. Lessons were inexpensive but his work commitments were immovable which meant it was unfortunately impractical to get to the lessons. He was disappointed.

How did you do?

The consonant l

There are two rules to remember when using the consonant **l**.

Rule 1

At the end of words of one syllable, you double the **l**.

fall

Rule 2

When words sound like they end in *–ful*, *–al* or *–ul*, there is only one **l**. Words with an **all** sound at the beginning, also only have one **l**.

Always be careful not to have an accidental fall!

all + ways = always

care + full = careful

accident + all = accidental

Warm up

1 Write these words out correctly in full adding the correct **l** ending.

a) ca_____

b) ha_____

c) ba_____

d) care_____

e) wonder_____

f) te_____

g) mi_____

h) tropic_____

i) power_____

j) grate_____

k) fu_____

2 Rewrite each word correctly.

allways	**allmost**
allone	**allready**
allthough	**allmighty**

3 Take the **–al** suffix off each word. Write the root word you are left with.

comical	**seasonal**
national	**musical**
regional	**topical**
tropical	**logical**

Challenge yourself

4 Correctly add **–full** to each of these words.
Use Rule 2 to help you.

use	**hope**
power	**cheer**
help	**pain**
rest	**thank**

5 Choose three of the words from question 4 above. Write a sentence for each word.

The suffixes -cious and -tious

Very few common words end with **–cious** or **–tious**. They give a **shus** sound when added to a root word.

Examples:

spa**ce** – spa**cious**

When the root word ends in **–ce**, the **ce** is dropped and **–cious** is added.

ficti**on** – ficti**tious**

Root words ending in other letters usually have **–tious** added.

Warm up

1. Write out the pairs of words that contain the same root words. Underline the common root in both.

   An example has been done for you.

   a) space   malicious

   b) caution   spacious

   c) grace   fictitious

   d) malice   vicious

   e) infect   gracious

   f) ambition   cautious

   g) vice   ambitious

   h) fiction   infectious

2 What are the missing words? Write them out in full.

m	a	l	i	c			s	
	m							
	b							
v	i			o	u	s		c
								a
f		c	t	i				u	s
								i
	s							o

Challenge yourself

3 Choose an appropriate word from the box to complete each sentence. Decide whether it needs a suffix added to it to turn it into an adjective to complete the sentence.

space   suspicion   envy   grace   caution
fiction   infection   nutrition   continue

a) The book was a work of _____.

b) He prepared a very _____ meal.

c) They applauded and were _____ in defeat.

d) The doctor wore a mask to prevent _____.

e) They were _____ of the stranger.

f) The children used great _____ when crossing the road.

g) Sam was very _____ of Amir's new car.

h) The band played _____ music all afternoon.

i) It was incredible _____ inside the tent.

How did you do?

Adding suffixes to –fer words

Words ending in **–fer** have two rules when adding suffixes that begin with vowels, e.g. **–er**, **–ing**, **–ence**.

Rule 1:	Rule 2:
infer – infe**rr**ed	prefer – prefe**r**ence
prefer – prefe**rr**ing	refer – refe**r**ence
The **r** is doubled if the **–fer** is stressed after the suffix has been added.	The **r** is not doubled if the **–fer** is not stressed after the suffix has been added.

1 Write out these words in the past tense by adding **–ed**. Decide whether you need to double the final **r**.

prefer	**buffer**
refer	**transfer**
infer	**confer**

2 Identify the words that can have **–ing** added to them without doubling the **r**.

transfer	**differ**
occur	**offer**
suffer	**prefer**

3 Identify the **three** misspelled words and write each one using its correct spelling.

referrence	**offering**	**suffered**	**refered**
transferred	**preferrence**	**occurring**	**suffered**

Challenge yourself

4 Write a sentence for each given word.

Use a dictionary to help you.

a) transferring

b) preferring

c) suffering

d) inferring

e) conferred

f) offered

g) deferred

h) differing

i) referring

j) proffered

How did you do?

Homophones 1

Many confusing words are **homophones** or **near-homophones** – they are spelt differently, but sound very similar.

For example, these are near-homophones.

device
a noun

devise
a verb

In such pairs of words, nouns often end with **ce** and verbs with **se**.

It is useful to remember that in pairs of words such as **device** and **devise**, the verb is pronounced with a **z** sound. This cannot be spelt with a **c**.

Warm up

1 Use a dictionary to help you to write a definition for each of these near-homophones.

a) advice

b) advise

c) device

d) devise

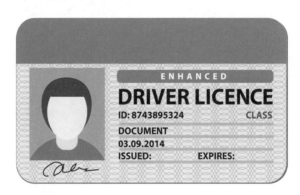

e) licence

f) license

g) practice

h) practise

2 Look at these nouns.
For each noun, write the verb (with the **se** ending).
Then write a sentence containing either the verb or the noun.

a) advice

b) device

c) licence

d) practice

Challenge yourself

3 Use a dictionary to find out the meaning of the words **prophecy** and **prophesy**.

Then write a sentence containing each word.

4 The following homophones use either **s** or **c** to give the **s** sound as in snake.

Find a definition for each homophone, then write a sentence for each word, making sure you use the correct context.

a) cellar / seller

b) cereal / serial

c) sent / cent

d) insight / incite

e) cede / seed

f) cite / site

How did you do?

Progress test 1

Choose the correct spelling and write it down.

1 fashionable / fashionible

2 unique / younique

3 carefull / careful

4 cautious / caushus

5 occurring / occuring

Write the correct spelling for each word.

6 transfered

7 flexable

8 fictishus

9 preferr

10 thankfull

Write the correct spelling for each underlined word.

11 The amount of litter was <u>deplorible</u>.

12 Each recruit looked smart in their new <u>youniform</u>.

13 There was a danger she could slip and <u>fal</u> from the branch.

14 He should have listened to his own <u>advise</u>.

15 The teacher told the choir to <u>practice</u> their singing.

16 – 20 Read the passage below. Find the **five** incorrect spellings and then write the correct spelling of each word.

> He had allready got a powerfull trycicle but now he desperately wanted a reliarbul bycycle to use for his daily commute to school.

Score ⬤/ 20

Choose the correct spelling and write it down.

1 youniverse / universe

2 triangle / tryangle

3 ambishus / ambitious

4 suitable / suitible

5 gracious / grass's

Write the correct spelling for each word.

6 invisable

7 infectshus

8 referal

9 cheerfull

10 vishus

Write the correct spelling for each underlined word.

11 The colourful kites were a <u>remarkible</u> sight.

12 She used a <u>trypod</u> to hold the camera steady.

13 It <u>allways</u> seemed to be raining.

14 Most of the customers seemed to be <u>prefferring</u> the fresh food.

15 The dentist opened a new <u>practise</u> in the town.

16 – **20** Read the passage below. Find the **five** incorrect spellings and then write the correct spelling of each word.

> They were very surspishus that their neighbour was stealing the valuble and preshus tropicil fish so they installed a fantastic devise to survey the pond.

Score ◯ / 20

17

The suffixes –cial and –tial

The word ending pronounced **shul** commonly uses **–cial** after a vowel and **–tial** after a consonant.

Examples:

offi**cial**

confiden**tial**

There are exceptions that you have to learn. These include **initial**, **financial**, **commercial** and **provincial**.

Warm up

1 Add either the suffix **–cial** or **–tial** to each word, writing the word in full.

offi

spe

essen

confiden

artifi

par

2 Write a definition for each of the following words.

Use a dictionary to help you.

a) financial

b) commercial

c) provincial

3 Write out and match the word families.

An example has been done for you.

a) confidential	office	financier
b) special	finance	confidence
c) official	part	speciality
d) financial	confident	partially
e) partial	specialise	officer

4 Write a sentence containing each given word.

a) artificial

b) essential

c) initial

d) confidential

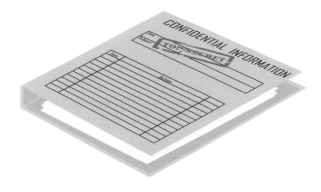

e) special

f) official

How did you do?

Words ending in –ate and –ite

The endings **–ate** and **–ite** are quite common.

Example:

The pir**ate** was not very pol**ite**!

You have to learn which ending to use.

Warm up

1 Write out these words in full with the correct ending, **–ate** or **–ite**.
Use a dictionary to help you.

priv	**rec**
favour	**decor**
inv	**chocol**
consider	**defin**
ign	**clim**

2 Write a sentence containing each pair of words.

a) favourite   chocolate

b) decorate   private

3 Identify the three misspelled words and write each one using its correct spelling.

investigate	**privite**
opposite	**considerate**
favourate	**educate**
create	**certificite**

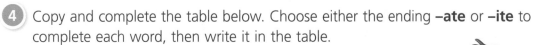
Challenge yourself

4 Copy and complete the table below. Choose either the ending **–ate** or **–ite** to complete each word, then write it in the table.

investig	**exc**	**exquis**
desper	**fortun**	**irrit**
dynam	**oppos**	**favour**
defin	**infl**	**illustr**
separ	**pol**	**appet**

–ate words	–ite words

How did you do?

Singular and plural rule-breakers

The spelling of most nouns follows simple rules when you write their plural forms. However, some nouns do not stick to the rules!

Example:

You can say:

one house and two house**s**

However, you should **not** say:

one mouse and two mouses

Warm up

1. Copy and match up the singular and plural forms of these nouns. Remember some words have the same singular and plural form.

   An example has been done for you.

singular	plural	singular	plural
mouse	teeth	child	deer
goose	feet	person	people
man	mice	louse	fish
tooth	oxen	sheep	women
ox	aircraft	fish	lice
aircraft	men	deer	sheep
foot	geese	woman	children

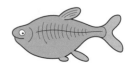

Answers

Pages 4–5

1. fashionable, invisible, responsible, suitable, reasonable, remarkable, horrible, flexible
2. value, rely, deplore, move, memory, use
3. **Words to be identified and written correctly in any order:** reasonable, memorable, responsible
4. a) leak   b) assist   c) giant
   d) mountain   e) family   f) sign
   g) just   h) rely
   Sentences will vary, but they must contain the stated word with the correct spelling, must be correctly punctuated and must make sense.

Pages 6–7

1. tricycle, unicycle, bicycle
2. a) unicorn – a mythical white horse with one horn
   b) unison – everyone singing the same one note
   c) unify – to make into one
   d) unique – the only one of its kind
   e) biplane – an aircraft with two sets of wings
   f) binoculars – two tubes next to each other, each containing lenses for viewing distant objects
   g) triplets – three siblings born at the same time
   h) triathlon – a sporting event in which competitors complete three disciplines
   i) tripod – a stand with three legs
3. a) bisect   b) bilingual
   c) biped   d) bicycle
4. a) triple   b) triangle
   c) trio   d) tricycle
5. **Words to be identified and written in any order:** impossible – possible, unicycle – cycle, incapable – capable, bicycle – cycle, inexpensive – expensive, immovable – movable, unfortunately – fortunately, impractical – practical, disappointed – appointed

Pages 8–9

1. a) call   b) hall   c) ball
   d) careful   e) wonderful   f) tell
   g) mill   h) tropical   i) powerful
   j) grateful   k) full
2. always, almost, alone, already, although, almighty
3. comic, season, nation, music, region, topic, tropic, logic
4. useful, hopeful, powerful, cheerful, helpful, painful, restful, thankful
5. **Sentences will vary, but each must contain a word from activity 4 with the correct spelling. Each sentence must be correctly punctuated and must make sense.**

Pages 10–11

1. a) space / spacious
   b) caution / cautious
   c) grace / gracious
   d) malice / malicious
   e) infect / infectious
   f) ambition / ambitious
   g) vice / vicious
   h) fiction / fictitious
2. **Across:** malicious, vicious, fictitious
   Down: ambitious, cautious
3. a) fiction   b) nutritious   c) gracious
   d) infection   e) suspicious   f) caution
   g) envious   h) continuous   i) spacious

Pages 12–13

1. preferred, buffered, referred, transferred, inferred, conferred
2. differ, offer, suffer
3. **Words to be identified and written correctly in any order:** reference, referred, preference
4. a)–j) **Sentences will vary, but they must contain the stated word with the correct spelling, must be correctly punctuated and must make sense.**

Pages 14–15

1. a) advice – an opinion or recommendation given to somebody
   b) advise – to give advice
   c) device – something made for a particular purpose
   d) devise – to make a plan or develop an idea
   e) licence – a document giving the holder permission to do something
   f) license – the permission to do something
   g) practice – a habit or the repetition of a skill to become more proficient
   h) practise – to repeatedly do something to become better at it
2. a) advise   b) devise
   c) license   d) practise
   Sentences will vary, but they must contain the verb or noun with the correct spelling, must be correctly punctuated and must make sense.
3. prophecy – (noun) a prediction of the future; prophesy – (verb) to predict something
   Sentences will vary, but they must contain the stated word with the correct spelling, must be correctly punctuated and must make sense.
4. **Sentences will vary, but they must contain the stated word with the correct spelling, be correctly punctuated and make sense.**

Page 16

1. fashionable
2. unique
3. careful
4. cautious
5. occurring

Answers

6. transferred
7. flexible
8. fictitious
9. prefer
10. thankful
11. deplorable
12. uniform
13. fall
14. advice
15. practise
16–20. **The following five words can be written in any order:** already, powerful, tricycle, reliable, bicycle

Page 17
1. universe
2. triangle
3. ambitious
4. suitable
5. gracious
6. invisible
7. infectious
8. referral
9. cheerful
10. vicious
11. remarkable
12. tripod
13. always
14. preferring
15. practice
16–20. **The following five words can be written in any order:** suspicious, valuable, precious, tropical, device

Pages 18–19
1. official, confidential, special, artificial, essential, partial
2. a) financial – related to money and finance
   b) commercial – related to commerce and business
   c) provincial – local or related to a province
3. a) confidential – confident – confidence
   b) special – specialise – speciality
   c) official – office – officer
   d) financial – finance – financier
   e) partial – part – partially
4. a)–f) **Sentences will vary, but they must contain the stated word with the correct spelling, must be correctly punctuated and must make sense.**

Pages 20–21
1. private, recite, favourite, decorate, invite, chocolate, considerate, definite, ignite, climate
2. a)–b) **Sentences will vary, but they must contain the stated words with the correct spelling, must be correctly punctuated and must make sense.**

3. **Words to be identified and written correctly in any order:** private, favourite, certificate
4. **–ate words:** investigate, desperate, fortunate, irritate, inflate, illustrate, separate
   –ite words: excite, exquisite, dynamite. opposite, favourite, definite, polite, appetite

Pages 22–23
1. mouse – mice; goose – geese; man – men; tooth – teeth;
   ox – oxen; aircraft – aircraft; foot – feet; child – children; person – people; louse – lice; sheep – sheep; fish – fish;
   deer – deer; woman – women
2. a)–f) **Sentences will vary, but they must include 'women', 'mice', 'children', 'sheep', 'people' and 'fish' with the correct spelling, must be correctly punctuated and must make sense.**
3. cacti / cactuses, oases, media, gateaux, formulae, fungi, larvae, radiuses / radii, plateaux, crises

Pages 24–25
1. primary, aeroplane, aquarium, audience, subway, expel, conjunction, supersonic
2. a) amo / amiable
   b) corpus / corpse
   c) dentis / dental
   d) moveo / movement
   e) pendeo / pendulum
   f) tempus / temporary
   g) sedeo / reside
   h) caput / captain
   i) curro / current
   j) manus / manufacture
   k) poena / penalty
   l) verbum / proverb
3. **Answers will vary but words could include:** vis – vision, visual, visor, television; scrib – scribble, scribe, scribing, describe, description; sig – signature, sign, signal, signing, significant

Pages 26–27
1. **Answers will vary, but they could include:** antiseptic, archbishop, autograph, parallel, telephone, microphone, photograph, diameter
2. **Words to be identified and written correctly in any order:** telephone, geography, architect
3. a) aster – astrology   b) grapho – autograph
   c) logos – dialogue   d) pathos – pathetic
   e) polis – politics   f) gramma – grammar
   g) sphaira – sphere   h) bios – biology
   i) kosmos – cosmetic   j) metron – metre
   k) phone – microphone   l) skopeo – telescope
   m) oide – melody   n) optikus – optician

Answers

Pages 28–29

1. duvet, trumpet, cricket, cabaret, ballet, scarlet, bracket, bouquet, ticket, buffet
2. **ay sound:** duvet, cabaret, ballet, bouquet, buffet
   et sound: trumpet, cricket, scarlet, bracket, ticket
3. **a)** ballet **b)** cabaret **c)** duvet
4. **a)–g) Sentences will vary, but they must contain the stated word with the correct spelling, must be correctly punctuated and must make sense.**

Page 30

1. official
2. climate
3. opposite
4. machine
5. sachet
6. commercial
7. separate
8. definite
9. telephone
10. cricket
11. essential
12. desperate
13. illustrate
14. people
15. parachute
16–20. **The following five words can be written in any order:** investigation, substantial, photographs, chef, artificial

Page 31

1. private
2. polite
3. audience
4. duvet
5. souvenir
6. confidential
7. invite
8. aquarium
9. primary
10. brochure
11. special
12. climate
13. irritate
14. ballet
15. dialogue
16–20. **The following five words can be written in any order:** decorate, chocolate, children, favourite, buffet

Pages 32–33

1. **a)** observant – observation – observance
   b) expectant – expectation – expectancy
   c) hesitant – hesitate – hesitation
   d) tolerant – tolerate – tolerance
   e) substance – substantial – substantially

2. expectance, expectant, hesitance, hesitant, substance
3. expectant / expectancy; hesitant / hesitancy; flamboyant / flamboyancy; reluctant / reluctancy
4. hesitancy / hesitance; reluctancy / reluctance; relevancy / relevance; expectancy / expectance
5. **a)** expectant
   b) observant
   c) hesitant
   d) flamboyant

Pages 34–35

1. **a)** innocent – innocence – innocently
   b) decent – decency – decently
   c) frequent – frequence – frequently
   d) confident – confidence – confidential
   e) obedient – obedience – obediently
2. **a)** confident – having a strong belief that something will happen
   b) obedient – obeying an order or wish directed at you
   c) innocent – having done nothing wrong
3. innocence / innocent; frequence / frequent; difference / different; confidence / confident; independence / independent
4. **a)–f) Sentences will vary, but they must contain the stated word with the correct spelling, must be correctly punctuated and must make sense.**

Pages 36–37

1. **a)** –en: quicken, soften, brighten, lighten
   b) –er: boxer, printer, teacher, gardener
2. fat, shave, white, worry
3. witchcraft – woodcraft; northern – eastern; wholesome – tiresome; playwright – wheelwright; backward – homeward; artful – merciful; warlike – lifelike; lengthwise – otherwise; childish – foolish
4. **Sentences will vary, but each must contain a word from question 3 which must have the correct spelling, be correctly punctuated and must make sense.**

Pages 38–39

1. **a)** Tuesday **b)** Friday **c)** Thursday
   d) Sunday **e)** Saturday **f)** Monday
2. **a)** August **b)** May **c)** January
   d) July **e)** June
3. **a)** September **b)** October
   c) November **d)** December
4. **a)** biro – a ballpoint pen. Named after the inventor of the ballpoint pen, Laszlo Biro.
   b) diesel – a type of fuel. Named after Rudolf Diesel, who invented the diesel engine.
   c) pasteurise – a process to prolong the life of food. Named after Louis Pasteur, the French microbiologist.

Answers

d) achilles – a tendon in the heel. Named after Achilles, a Greek warrior who was killed when wounded in his heel.

e) morse code – a system of long and short sounds or flashes of light used for sending messages. Named after Samuel Morse who invented this system.

Pages 40–41

1. **a)** stationary – to be still; stationery – writing materials

b) principle – a rule or code of conduct; principal – highest rank in a system, e.g. principal of a school (the head teacher)

c) profit – a gain in money; prophet – a person who speaks on behalf of a god

d) morning – the first part of the day; mourning – an act of sorrow following a death

2. paws – pause
steel – steal
wary – weary
principal – principle
herd – heard
affect – effect
altar – alter
piece – peace
aloud – allowed
practice – practise

3. compliment – an expression of praise
complement – when something goes well with something else
Sentences will vary, but they must contain the stated word with the correct spelling, must be correctly punctuated and must make sense.

4. **a)** guest / their
b) allowed / cellar
c) steal / altar
d) morning / peace
e) plain / knows
f) paws / scent

Page 42

1. innocence
2. brighten
3. December
4. hesitant
5. decency
6. August
7. obediently
8. intelligence
9. observant
10. confidently
11. independence
12. whiten
13. pasteurised
14. stationery
15. grate
16–20. **The following five words can be written in any order:** freedom, frequent, worrier, Thursday, profit

Page 43

1. quicken
2. November
3. woollen
4. relevance
5. reluctant
6. confidence
7. January
8. kingdom
9. innocently
10. tolerant
11. soften
12. diesel
13. stationary
14. isle
15. complement
16–20. **The following five words can be written in any order:** great, playwright, pause, mourners, compliments

2 Write sentences containing the plural form of the given words.

a) woman

b) mouse

c) child

d) sheep

e) person

f) fish

Challenge yourself
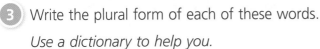

3 Write the plural form of each of these words.
Use a dictionary to help you.

cactus	**oasis**
medium	**gateau**
formula	**fungus**
larva	**radius**
plateau	**crisis**

How did you do?

Latin words

Many words, or parts of words, in the English language come from Latin.

> **Example:**
>
> **manus** means **hand** in Latin. The words below come from it.
>
>
>
> **manu**facture
>
>
>
> **manu**script

Warm up

1 Many prefixes come from Latin.

Look at the words below and identify their correct place in the table.

An example has been done for you.

aquarium	primary	subway	audience
supersonic	expel	aeroplane	conjunction

Latin prefix	meaning	word that includes the prefix
prim–	first	primary
aero–	air	
aqua–	water	
audi–	hearing	
sub–	under	
ex–	out	
con–	together	
super–	above	

2 Copy and match these Latin words with the related words from modern English.
An example has been done for you.

a) amo (I love) ——————————————— dental

b) corpus (body) amiable

c) dentis (tooth) current

d) moveo (I move) manufacture

e) pendeo (I hang) reside

f) tempus (time) captain

g) sedeo (I sit) corpse

h) caput (head) penalty

i) curro (I run) proverb

j) manus (hand) temporary

k) poena (punishment) pendulum

l) verbum (word) movement

Challenge yourself

3 Consider the origins of **vis**, **scrib** and **sig** as used in **vision**, **scribble** and **signature**.
Write a few related words for each one.

a) vis words

b) scrib words

c) sig words

Greek words

Many words, or parts of words, in the English language come from the Ancient Greek.

Example: the Greek word **tele** means **from afar**.

The word **telephone** actually means **sound from afar**.

Warm up

1 Many prefixes come from Greek. Think of a word for each prefix to complete the table.

An example has been done for you.

Use a dictionary to help you.

Greek prefix	meaning	word that includes the prefix
anti–	against	antiseptic
arch–	chief	
auto–	self	
para–	beside	
tele–	from afar	
micro–	small	
photo–	light	
dia–	through	

2 Identify the **three** misspelled words and write each one using its correct spelling.

microscope	**teliphone**	**autograph**	**jography**
phonics	**parachute**	**arcitect**	**astronomy**

Challenge yourself

3 Copy and match these Greek words with the related words from modern English. An example has been done for you.

a) aster (star) ——————————————— cosmetic

b) grapho (I write) ——— astrology

c) logos (word/speech)   dialogue

d) pathos (suffering)   telescope

e) polis (city)   pathetic

f) gramma (thing written)   biology

g) sphaira (globe)   autograph

h) bios (life)   melody

i) kosmos (beauty)   sphere

j) metron (a measure)   optician

k) phone (sound)   politics

l) skopeo (I see)   grammar

m) oide (a song)   metre

n) optikus (to do with sight)   microphone

How did you do?

French Words

A lot of words used in English have been borrowed from the French language. Many words taken from French contain the letters **ch**.

> **Example:**
>
>
>
> A **chef** works in a restaurant.

Words ending **–et** also often indicate that a word comes from French.

 Warm up

1 Rewrite the incomplete words below with an **–et** ending.

duv_____   trump_____

crick_____   cabar_____

ball_____   scarl_____

brack_____   bouqu_____

tick_____   buff_____

2 Say aloud the words you have made in question 1 above. Then copy and complete the table below, adding the words to the correct column.

Two examples have been done for you.

–et sounds like *ay* as in day	–et sounds like *et* as in wet
duvet	trumpet

3 Which **–et** word from question 1 on page 28 means:

a) a type of dance?

b) a variety of entertainments?

c) a bed covering?

Challenge yourself

4 Read aloud the words below and listen to the sound the **ch** makes. Then write a sentence for each given word.

a) parachute

b) chef

c) brochure

d) sachet

e) machine

f) chandelier

g) quiche

Choose the correct spelling and write it down.

1 offichal / official

2 climait / climate

3 opposite / opposit

4 machine / mashine

5 sashet / sachet

Write the correct spelling for each word.

6 commerchal

7 seperate

8 defenite

9 tellyfone

10 crickeat

Write the correct spelling for each underlined word.

11 The <u>essenshall</u> ingredient was a secret.

12 The children were <u>desperite</u> to build a sandcastle.

13 She could <u>illuschrate</u> three books per week.

14 All of the <u>persons</u> on the bus were going to the shops.

15 It would be his first ever <u>parashoot</u> jump.

16 – 20 Read the passage below. Find the **five** incorrect spellings and then write the correct spelling of each word.

> **The investigayshen promised a substanchal reward for photografs of the shef using artifishell products in his kitchen.**

Score ◯ / 20

Choose the correct spelling and write it down.

1 privit / private

2 polight / polite

3 ordience / audience

4 duvet / doovay

5 souvenir / soovaneer

Write the correct spelling for each word.

6 confidentchal

7 invight

8 akwarium

9 primery

10 broshure

Write the correct spelling for each underlined word.

11 Speshul gifts arrived from all over the world.

12 The scientists were concerned about climit change.

13 She knew how to iritate her big brother.

14 The whole class had ballee lessons with the dance teacher.

15 The story contained lots of dialog.

16 – 20 Read the passage below. Find the **five** incorrect spellings and then write the correct spelling of each word.

> **Dad was busy trying to decoraight the chocolet cake. All the childs said it was their faverate so it just had to be on the buffay for the party.**

Score ⬤ / 20

The suffixes -ant, -ance and -ancy

The suffixes, **–ant**, **–ance** or **–ancy** can often be added to the same root.

Examples:

The man was hesit**ant**.

He hesitates for a moment.

His hesit**ance** cost him vital seconds,

His hesit**ancy** was costly.

Warm up

1 Write out and match the word families. An example has been done for you.

a) observant	hesitate	observance
b) expectant	expectation	hesitation
c) hesitant	observation	tolerance
d) tolerant	substantial	expectancy
e) substance	tolerate	substantially

2 Rewrite this list of words in alphabetical order.

expectant

hesitant

substance

hesitance

expectance

3 Copy and complete the table below, and replace the **–ant** endings with **–ancy** endings.

An example has been done for you.

–ant ending	–ancy ending
expectant	expectancy
hesitant	
flamboyant	
reluctant	

4 Copy and complete the table with the correct **–ance** endings.

An example has been done for you.

–ancy ending	–ance ending
hesitancy	hesitance
reluctancy	
relevancy	
expectancy	

Challenge yourself

5 Read the sentences below and choose the best word to add.
Each word will need changing to its correct form.

Use a dictionary to help you.

flamboyancy   **expect**   **hesitate**   **observe**

a) The _____ mother was preparing for her new baby.

b) They were very _____ to spot that the painting was a fake.

c) He was _____ because he did not know what lay beyond.

d) The band wore very _____ clothes.

How did you do?

–ent and –ence endings

The **–ent** or **–ence** ending is often used if a word has a soft *c*, a soft *g* or a *qu* sound, or when a related word has a clear **e** sound near the end.

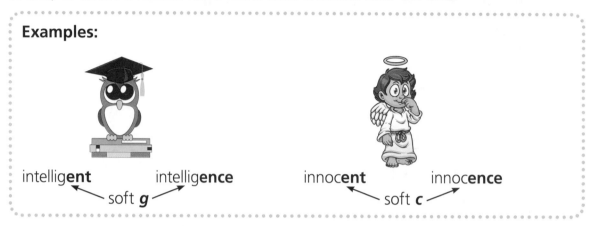

Examples:

intellig**ent**   intellig**ence**   innoc**ent**   innoc**ence**

soft **g**   soft **c**

Unfortunately this is not a rule. There are many words which use **–ent** or **–ence**, but do not follow the above rule. You just have to learn them.

Warm up

1   Write out and match the word families.

An example has been done for you.

a) innocent	decency	confidential
b) decent	frequence	decently
c) frequent	confidence	obediently
d) confident	innocence	frequently
e) obedient	obedience	innocently

2   Write the definition of each of these words.

Use a dictionary to help you.

a) confident

b) obedient

c) innocent

3 Copy and complete the table with the correct **–ent** endings.

An example has been done for you.

–ence ending	–ent ending
innocence	innocent
frequence	
difference	
confidence	
independence	

4 Write a sentence containing each given word.

a) difference

b) independent

c) frequent

d) confidence

e) innocence

f) obedient

How did you do?

Anglo-Saxon suffixes

Many suffixes also originate from the Anglo-Saxon period of history.

Examples:

darken

The suffix **–en** can mean **to make**. Dark**en** therefore means to make dark.

drumm**er**

The suffix **–er** often means a do**er** of something. A drumm**er** is therefore someone who drums.

Sometimes the spelling of the root word stays the same when the suffix is added.

Sometimes the spelling of the root word is changed slightly when the suffix is added.

Warm up

1 **a)** Turn these adjectives into verbs by adding the suffixe **–en**.

quick   soft

bright   light

b) Turn these verbs into nouns by adding the suffix **–er**.

box   print

teach   garden

2 Take the suffix off these words, and work out the root words.

fatten   shaven

whiten   worrier

3 Here are some more words with common Anglo-Saxon suffixes.

Write the pairs of words according to their suffixes. Then underline the common suffix in each word. An example has been done for you.

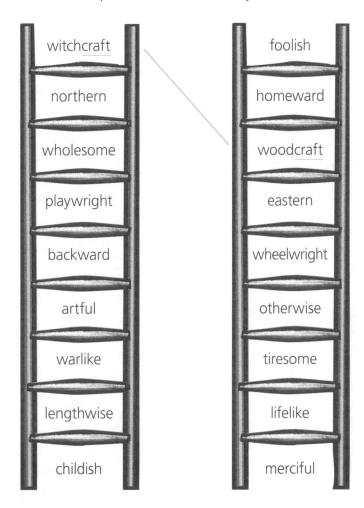

witchcraft

northern

wholesome

playwright

backward

artful

warlike

lengthwise

childish

foolish

homeward

woodcraft

eastern

wheelwright

otherwise

tiresome

lifelike

merciful

4 Choose three of the words from the ladders above. Write a sentence for each word.

Use a dictionary to help you.

How did you do?

The history of words

Some English words have fascinating histories! Understanding a little about the origins of words may help you to remember them better.

Examples:

Wednesday

This day is named after Woden, a Viking god.

March

This month is named after Mars, the Roman god of war.

Warm up

1 Which day do you think was named after:

a) Tiw, a Viking god?

b) Frig, a Viking goddess?

c) Thor, a god of thunder?

d) the Sun?

e) Saturn, a Roman god?

f) the Moon?

2 Which month do you think was named after:

a) the Roman Emperor Augustus?

b) Maia, the Roman goddess of spring?

c) Janus, a two-faced god?

d) the Roman Emperor Julius Caesar?

e) the chief Roman goddess, Juno?

3 Write which month you think comes from each of these Roman numbers.

a) septem (seven)

b) octo (eight)

c) novem (nine)

d) decem (ten)

Challenge yourself

Eponyms are words that have originated from people's names. For example, the guillotine is named after Dr Joseph Guillotin.

4 Write the meaning of each of these words.
Can you find out how each word originated?

a) biro

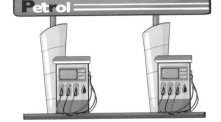

b) diesel

c) pasteurise

d) achilles

e) morse code

How did you do?

Homophones 2

In your reading and writing, you should have encountered a number of **homophones** and **near-homophones**. Remember that they are words that sound the same or similar, but have a different spelling.

Here are some examples:

grate	great
nose	knows
steel	steal
plane	plain
aisle	isle
bridle	bridal

plane

plain

bridle

bridal

Warm up

1. Look at each pair of homophones and write a definition for each word.

   a) stationary / stationery

   b) principle / principal

   c) profit / prophet

   d) morning / mourning

2 Identify the pairs of homophones and near-homophones from the list below.

paws	steel	wary	principal
herd	pause	heard	steal
affect	altar	weary	alter
piece	aloud	practise	allowed
practice	effect	principle	peace

Challenge yourself

3 What is the difference between the words **compliment** and **complement**? Write a definition for each word, followed by a sentence containing the word.

4 Using your knowledge of homophones, find the **two** words that have been used incorrectly in each sentence. Then write the homophones that should replace them.

a) It was a pleasure to be a guessed in there house.

b) Nobody was aloud in the seller.

c) The thief tried to steel the chalice from the church alter.

d) My mum always gets up early in the mourning, so that she can have a cup of tea in piece.

e) It is plane to see that nobody nose where the treasure is hidden.

f) The dog licked his pause and then set-off, following the sent of the escaped prisoner.

How did you do?

Progress test 5

Choose the correct spelling and write it down.

1 innocense / innocence

2 brightern / brighten

3 December / Desember

4 hesitent / hesitant

5 desency / decency

Write the correct spelling for each word.

6 Augast

7 obydiently

8 intelligance

9 observont

10 confidenterly

Write the correct spelling for each underlined word.

11 Their <u>independance</u> helped them become confident and strong.

12 The dentist used a special paste to <u>whitern</u> teeth.

13 Milk is safe to drink if it is <u>pastarised</u>.

14 They went to the <u>stationary</u> shop to buy paper and pens.

15 Logs burned slowly in the fire <u>great</u>.

16 – 20 Read the passage below. Find the **five** incorrect spellings and then write the correct spelling of each word.

> Despite his freedum to do what he liked, he was a frequant worryer. Each Thurstday he would check how much prophet the shop was making.

Score ⬤ / 20

Choose the correct spelling and write it down.

1 quickan / quicken

2 Nowvember / November

3 woollen / woolen

4 relevence / relevance

5 reluctant / reluctent

Write the correct spelling for each word.

6 confidance

7 Janruary

8 kingdum

9 innocantly

10 toleront

Write the correct spelling for each underlined word.

11 Chemicals can be used to <u>softern</u> materials.

12 The lorry used lots of <u>deisel</u> on its journey across Europe.

13 Cars were <u>stationery</u> for several hours in the traffic jam.

14 They lived on a small, windswept <u>aisle</u> off the Scottish coast.

15 As a chef he loved to cook foods that would <u>compliment</u> each other.

16 – **20** Read the passage below. Find the **five** incorrect spellings and then write the correct spelling of each word.

> At the funeral of the grate playright, there was a short paws before the morners paid their complements in a number of speeches.

Published by Keen Kite Books
An imprint of HarperCollins*Publishers* Ltd
The News Building
1 London Bridge Street
London SE1 9GF

ISBN 9780008161576

Text and design © 2015 Keen Kite Books, an imprint of HarperCollins*Publishers* Ltd

Author: Jon Goulding

The author asserts his moral right to be identified as the author of this work.